The Jesse Tree

An Advent Activity Book

Katie Thompson

Illustrated by Sara Walker

Kevin
Mayhew

First published in 1998 by
KEVIN MAYHEW LTD
Buxhall, Stowmarket
Suffolk IP14 3BW

9 8 7 6 5 4 3 2 1

ISBN 1 84003 230 8
Catalogue No. 1500217

Cover illustration by Sara Walker
Edited by Katherine Laidler
Typesetting by Louise Selfe

Printed in Great Britain

Contents

Introduction

Caesar Augustus, the Roman Emperor, ordered a census to be taken, and everyone returned to the town of their family origin to be registered. So it was that Joseph and Mary left Nazareth in Galilee and returned to Bethlehem in Judea, King David's boyhood home. All this came to pass because Joseph was a descendant of David's royal line . . . *(Luke 2:1-4)*

The Jesse tree provides a fun way to trace the 'royal roots' of Jesus, by discovering Christ's 'family tree' through biblical people associated historically, either through faith or bloodline, with the coming of the Messiah. This book offers an interesting and fresh presentation of a traditional idea, and has something to offer children and adults alike.

The image of the Jesse tree originates from the words of the prophet Isaiah:

A shoot will spring from the stock of Jesse, and from his roots a bud will blossom. *(Isaiah 11:1)*

The Jesse tree has become a tradition most often associated with Advent, and it develops gradually as the characters and stories unfold, reflecting the spirit of expectation so characteristic of this season.

This is a practical resource for children of school age, as well as for families wanting to add meaning to Advent amidst the glitz and glamour of Christmas. It is for groups working within a parish, and for schools searching for a new direction to take as they help young people to prepare for Christmas in an enjoyable and exciting way.

To make a Jesse tree you will need a Christmas tree or a dead tree-like branch. Whichever you choose, take care to make sure that it is securely anchored in a heavy pot or stand, filled with pebbles or damp sand. The Jesse tree is then ready to be brought to life! Week by week, symbols representing characters and events are added to the tree or branch; these are produced in a variety of ways depending on the time, resources, energy and ingenuity available!

As suggested here, the sixteen readings and their appropriate symbols can be split equally over the four Sundays of Advent, with four texts and activities being completed during each session. The symbols you choose and the way the material is used is, however, entirely flexible, and the ideas and suggestions can be adapted and developed to meet individual needs.

Wherever possible, materials which are readily available or easy to make have been used, and, with a little forward planning, many resources can be collected in advance during the year. Clear, illustrated instructions are given, and, where appropriate, templates for tracing or photocopying may be found in the section starting on page 59. You may need to plan ahead – for example, by making papier-mâché or salt dough apples a week in advance, so that they have time to dry thoroughly before they are painted in the first week of Advent. For the sake of safety you may also think about preparing beforehand some of the materials which require cutting and the making of holes, and always ensure that there are plenty of adults around to supervise younger children.

Biblical texts adapted for young people are given to explain each symbol, and ideas and suggestions for tree decorations which are practical and fun. The Jesse tree offers a wonderful way to find out more about the history of salvation for God's people, as we prepare to celebrate our Saviour's birth at Christmas.

KATIE THOMPSON

WEEK ONE

Adam and Eve
Noah and the flood
Abraham, father of God's people
The sacrifice of Isaac

Adam and Eve

While Adam and Eve were living happily together in the Garden of Eden, the devil, who loves to spoil the good things God has made, disguised himself as a snake and slithered up to Eve.

'Did God tell you not to eat any fruit from the trees in the garden?' he asked.

'Oh no,' she replied, 'we can pick fruit from anywhere except the tree in the middle of the garden. That fruit is forbidden, for if we eat it we will die.'

'Nonsense!' said the devil. 'God does not want you to eat that fruit because it will make you as wise as he is.'

The woman looked at the beautiful tree with its tempting fruits, and she wanted to be wise. So she picked a fruit and tasted it, and gave some to Adam. Later God came to the garden and called to Adam and Eve, but they hid from him because they were ashamed.

'Did you disobey me and eat the forbidden fruit?' God asked them.

'The snake made us do it, it was his fault,' answered Eve.

'No,' God said sadly. 'You chose to disobey me. Now you must leave this paradise, because your disobedience has allowed death to come into the world.'

God dressed them in animal skins and sent them from the garden out into the world.

Adapted from Genesis 3:1-24

The symbol of the Adam and Eve story is an apple, a fruit which represents disobedience to God. Adam and Eve wanted to be 'like God', and out of envy they were drawn towards what is wrong. They stopped trusting completely in God's goodness, and freely chose to disobey his command, committing humankind's first sin.

Artificial apple decorations which are both realistic and inexpensive are readily available from most stores providing Christmas decorations, and the run-up to Christmas is an ideal time to find a good selection.

Alternatively, you can make your own by choosing one of the four different methods described.

Apple 1

You will need . . .

Salt dough:
- 2 cups plain flour
- 1 cup salt
- 1 cup water
- Mixing bowl

- Cocktail stick
- Red and green acrylic paints
- Acrylic varnish (optional)
- Gold thread
- Green paper cut into leaf shapes
- Glue

Mix the flour, salt and half of the water in a bowl ①. Add the remaining water gradually ② and knead to a firm dough ③. If the dough feels sticky, add more flour and knead again for 10 minutes. Leave to 'rest' for 30 minutes in an airtight container or plastic bag before use.*

Mould the salt dough into apple shapes and carefully push a cocktail stick down through the 'core' of each fruit ④. To make your models last, bake them in an oven (250°F/120°C/Gas mark 1) until they become hard and sound hollow when tapped. When cool, paint them and add a final coat of clear varnish for a tough finish ⑤. When they are dry, fold a length of gold thread in half and knot the two ends together; pass the thread through the apple from bottom to top, so that the knot is at the bottom ⑥. After gluing the paper leaves into place on the apples ⑦, they are ready to hang on the tree.

* This dough can also be used to make the staff described in Method 2 on page 30.

Apple 2

You will need . . .

- Old tights
- Red crepe or tissue paper
- Scissors
- Glue
- Gold thread
- Double sided sellotape
- Green paper leaves

Roll a pair of old tights into a ball ②. Cut a circle of red crepe or tissue paper large enough to wrap tightly around the nylon ball and glue the paper into place as neatly as possible ④. A loop of gold thread can be sellotaped on to the apple to hang it from the tree ⑤. Stick some green paper leaves into place, and use a small roll of green paper to represent a stalk ⑦.

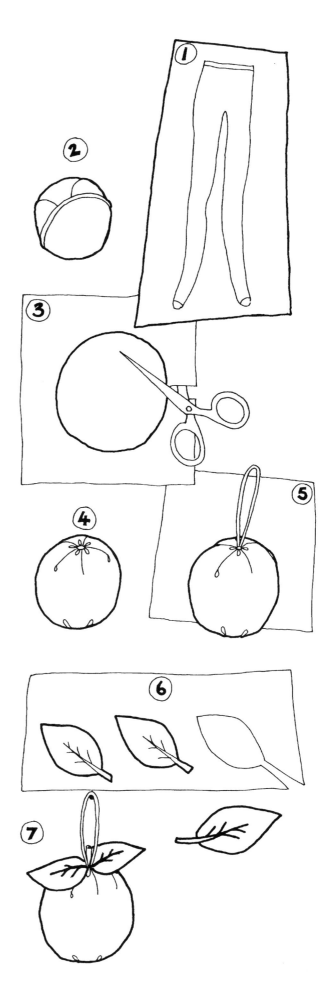

Apple 3

You will need . . .

- Newspapers
- Sellotape
- Gold thread
- Non-fungicidal wallpaper paste or flour and water paste
- Varnish
- Red and green poster paints
- Green paper (cut into a long strip and leaf shapes)
- Scissors

Crumple some newspaper into rough ball shapes and secure with sellotape ②. Tie a length of gold thread around the ball and make a loop for hanging ③. Tear strips of newspaper approximately 4 cm wide and 10 cm long ④. If you are using wallpaper paste, make it up according to the directions on the packet. If you are using flour and water paste, add a small amount of cold water to approximately 50-80 g of sieved plain white flour in a mixing bowl ⑤.

Mix gently to make a paste, and add enough water to achieve the consistency of thick batter. Dip the paper strips into the paste mixture and wrap them around your paper ball, leaving the loop clear for hanging. Change the direction you place the strips to give an even coverage ⑥. Use your fingers to smooth down the strips and wipe away any excess paste. When a satisfactory shape has been achieved, allow the apples to dry in a warm place, turning them frequently. When completely dry, paint with poster paints and varnish for extra strength ⑦. Roll a strip of green paper into a stalk shape and glue it into place at the top of the apple together with some paper leaves to add the finishing touch ⑨.

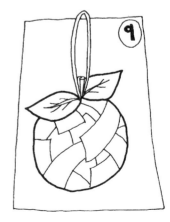

Apple 4

You will need . . .

- Thin card
- Red double knitting wool
- Scissors (sharp and pointed)
- Gold thread
- Green felt (or material)
- Latex adhesive or similar

Trace the circles template on page 59 and cut two from card. Hold the two pieces of card together, and begin to wind the red wool through the middle to hold them together ①. Continue to wind the wool evenly until the hole is almost completely filled ②. Using sharp pointed scissors, carefully snip through the wool all the way round the edges, until the card is visible ③. Take a length of gold thread, and slipping it between the two pieces of card, pull it tight and tie. Carefully remove the two pieces of card, and fluff up the wool into a pom-pom, before trimming if necessary. Tie the ends of the thread to make a loop, and glue on the felt or material leaves ④.

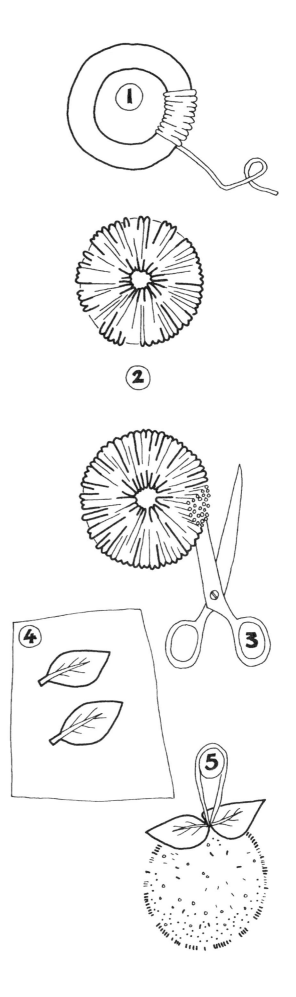

Noah and the flood

God looked down on the world he had made, and was filled with sadness when he saw the wickedness of the people. God decided to destroy all that was bad in his world, except for Noah who was a good and just man.

So God said to Noah, 'Build an ark and fill it with pairs of every sort of animal so that they will multiply again. Take plenty of food for them and your family, because I will send enough rain to flood the whole world.'

Noah listened well and did everything God had commanded. The rain began, and continued night and day, until all the land had disappeared beneath the mighty waters of the flood. Everything was destroyed, except for Noah and his family, and the animals which were safe in the ark.

After many days and nights, Noah sent out a dove which returned to the ark carrying a fresh olive shoot in its beak. Noah gave thanks and praise to God as the flood waters slowly began to disappear.

Then God said to Noah, 'I make a promise to you and all living creatures, that I will never again send such a flood to destroy the world. As a sign of this promise I will put a rainbow in the sky for everyone to see.'

Adapted from Genesis 6:9-8:11; 9:8-17

The story of the flood is intended to show Noah's faithfulness and trust in God. He did exactly what God asked him to do, and believed that God would take care of his family and all the creatures in the ark. God made a promise to Noah and his descendants – a universal promise which relates to all humankind. Even today a dove, like the one mentioned in the story, symbolises peace, love, hope and forgiveness. The symbols for Noah are an ark and a dove.

Ark

You will need . . .

- Thin card or corrugated cardboard
- Felt-tip pens
- Glue
- Hole punch or scissors
- Gold thread

Use the templates on page 59 to trace or photo-copy the rainbow and ark shapes on to the card. You will need two for each ark, so that they can be glued back to back. Do the same for the figure of Noah. Colour the ark and Noah, and position Noah on the deck between the two halves of the ark before gluing them together. Colour the rainbows, and glue matching pairs together. Use a hole punch or a pair of scissors to make holes through the top and middle of the rainbow arch and the roof of the ark. Loop some gold thread through the top of the rainbow for hanging from the tree, and attach the ark and the rainbow together using a short length of gold thread. If you want to make it more decorative, cut narrow strips of paper which can be folded to make 'windows'. Draw and colour pictures of animals inside, and glue them on to the ark to complete the scene.

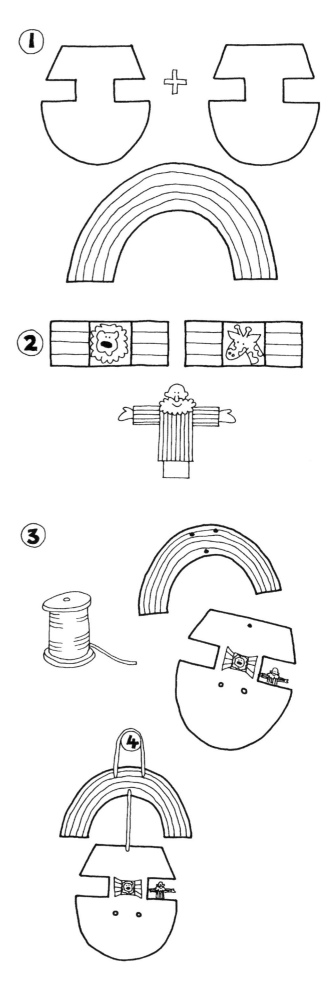

15

Dove

You will need . . .

- Thin white card
- Sheets of white paper
- Glue
- Sellotape
- Green card/paper or evergreen foliage (for example, leylandii)
- Gold thread

Use the template on page 60 to cut out a dove from white card ①. Fold a sheet of white paper like a fan ②. Carefully make a slit along the dotted line position and push the paper 'fan' through ③. Spread the fan carefully and secure the edges which meet with glue or sellotape above the middle of the dove ④. A small slit in the 'beak' can hold a small piece of fresh evergreen foliage or a piece of green card or paper cut in the shape of a leaf ⑤. Attach a loop of gold thread to the top of the wings and the dove is ready to hang.

Abraham, father of God's people

God spoke to Abraham in a dream: 'Abraham, do not be afraid, because I will take care of you and you shall have a great reward.'

Abraham answered him, 'Lord, what use is such a reward when I have no children to share it with?'

Then God told Abraham to go outside and look up at the night sky. 'Look at the stars, Abraham,' God said. 'See, there are too many to count. You will have as many descendants as there are stars in the sky.'

Abraham put his trust in God and believed everything he had heard, and God was pleased to see such faith.

Adapted from Genesis 15:1-6

Abraham was one of Noah's descendants and the first great biblical leader of the people of Israel. During Abraham's lifetime, a special trust grew between God and his family. Abraham was always ready to have faith in God and do whatever he asked, so God made a promise – or covenant – with Abraham and his descendants, that they would be his people and he would be their God. Abraham believed that he would have many descendants because he knew that nothing is impossible for God.

The symbols for Abraham are a star scene and individual figures of Abraham to hang from the tree.

Star scene

You will need . . .

- Thin card
- Felt-tip pens
- Self-adhesive gold or silver stars
- Hole punch or scissors
- Gold thread

Photocopy the Abraham scene on page 60 on to thin card and cut out ①. Colour Abraham and the background, making the sky dark blue or black. Add the self-adhesive stars to the sky to complete the scene ②. Colour the reverse side of the scene the same colour as the sky and cover with stars ③. Use a hole punch or pair of scissors to make a hole, and thread with a loop of gold thread to hang from the tree.

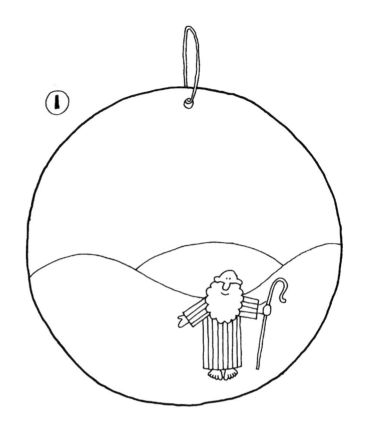

Abraham figure

You will need . . .

- White paper
- Scissors
- Felt-tip pens
- Flesh-coloured poster paint
- Cotton pulp balls, 20 mm diameter (available from any good craft shop), or pink tissue paper and cotton wool balls
- Corks
- Glue
- Scraps of coloured paper and material
- Striped non-woven kitchen cloths
- Narrow ribbon
- Black or brown pipe cleaners
- Gold thread

Use the template on page 60 to cut hands from white paper ②. Colour these pink using felt-tip pens or poster paints at the same time as the cotton balls. (Alternatively, wrap some pink tissue paper around a cotton wool ball and secure with sellotape.) When dry, take a pink ball and glue it to the end of a cork to make a head. Cover the cork by wrapping a piece of coloured paper or material around it, gluing the overlap at the back. Cut sleeves from the same paper or material and stick the hands on to the inside before gluing the sleeves into place on the body. Cut a beard from suitably coloured paper or material and glue it onto the head. Using the template on page 60, cut a piece of striped kitchen cloth to make the head-dress ②. Spread some glue on to the head and stick the cloth in place. Dot some glue inside the head-dress and press on to folds around the figure's body. A narrow piece of ribbon around the head completes the head-dress. Draw on eyes and a mouth, and glue a pipe cleaner shaped like a crook onto the inside of one hand ③. To hang the figure from the tree, glue or sellotape a loop of gold thread onto the head-dress.

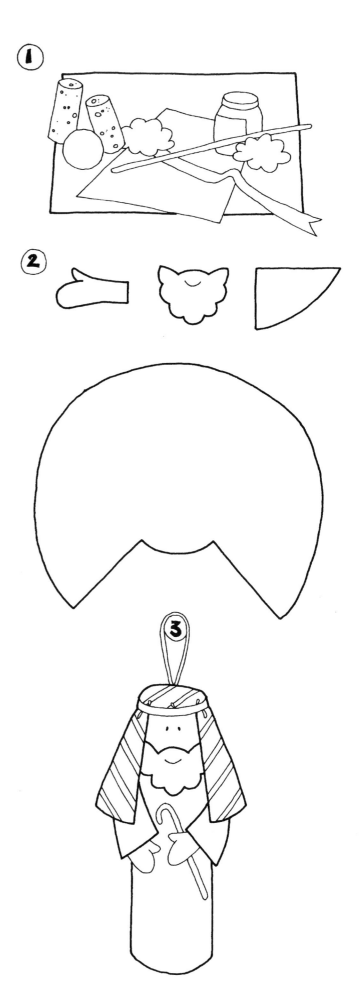

19

The sacrifice of Isaac

Although Abraham and his wife Sarah were both very old, Sarah gave birth to a son just as God had promised, because nothing is impossible for God. They called the boy Isaac, and they thanked God every day for the joy he brought them.

One day God put Abraham to the test. 'Abraham,' he said, 'I want you to take Isaac to the top of the mountain and offer him as a sacrifice to me.'

Abraham loved Isaac very much, but he trusted God completely and was ready to obey him. He loaded his donkey with wood and set off to the mountain God had shown him.

On the way, Isaac asked his father, 'Where is the lamb you will sacrifice?'

Abraham answered him, 'God will provide a lamb.'

When they arrived, they built an altar and piled it with wood. Then Abraham tied Isaac's hands and feet and took out a knife ready to kill his only son.

Suddenly a voice from heaven said, 'Abraham, Abraham, do not kill the son you love so much. Your love for me was so great that you were ready to sacrifice your only son for my sake.'

Adapted from Genesis 21:1-7; 22:1-12

Abraham's obedience to God was illustrated when he was asked to sacrifice his son, Isaac. He showed no hesitation in carrying out God's command, and demonstrated the depth of his love for God by his willingness to sacrifice his precious son. Isaac's symbol is a dagger. Lightweight, retractable plastic 'daggers' can be obtained inexpensively from most good toy shops, or you can make your own.

Dagger

You will need . . .

- Thin brown card or thin cardboard
- Thin white card
- Can of silver spray or roll of aluminium foil
- Glue
- Gold thread
- Coloured sequins or beads (optional)

Trace the blade and handle pattern on page 61 to make a card template. Fold the brown card or thin cardboard in two, and trace around the handle template against the fold (1). Now trace around the blade template on the white card (2). Spray the 'blades' silver, or wrap aluminium foil around them and glue. When dry, stick the silver blades inside the handles, attach a loop of gold thread at the opposite end and glue the handle halves together. Sequins or beads can be used to make the daggers more decorative (3).

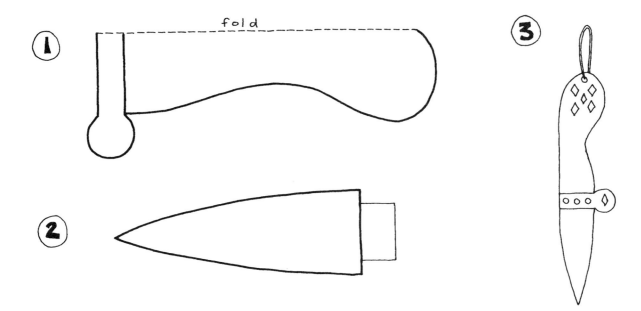

WEEK TWO

Jacob's ladder
Joseph feeds God's people
Moses leads the people out of Egypt
Moses and the Ten Commandments

Jacob's ladder

Jacob, the son of Isaac, set off for the town of Haran. When night fell, he set up camp and lay down to sleep, using a stone for his pillow. Once Jacob was asleep he began to dream. He saw a ladder reaching from the ground all the way up to heaven, and God's angels were making their way up and down it.

Then God spoke to Jacob. 'I am the God of Abraham and your father Isaac,' he said, 'and I give you and your descendants the land on which you lie. They will be as plentiful as the specks of dust on the ground, and spread far and wide across the land. Wherever you are, I will watch over and protect you.'

Then Jacob woke from his dream and he was filled with wonder. 'This place must be the gateway to heaven!' he exclaimed. 'God is present here and I had no idea until now.'

When morning came, Jacob got up early and used the stone that he had slept on to mark the holy place and he gave it the name 'Bethel', which means 'the house of God'.

Adapted from Genesis 28:10-22

Jacob was one of Isaac's sons, and his faith in God became even greater after his amazing dream. Jacob was given the name 'Israel' by God (Genesis 32:28-29 and 35:10), and so his descendants became known as the 'children of Israel'. Jacob's symbol on the tree is a ladder. A whole variety of materials can be used to make small ladders but, if you're stuck for time, most pet shops sell a variety of small plastic and wooden ladders in the cage bird section.

Ladders

You will need . . .

- Wooden kebab sticks (sharp ends trimmed off), pipe cleaners or thin card.
- String or wire bag fasteners
- Glue

For each ladder you need two identical lengths of sticks ① or pipe cleaners ②, and several shorter lengths to make the rungs. Use either the string or the wire fasteners to fasten each rung in place – don't worry about being too neat; they will look more authentic if they're a bit uneven! A simpler version uses strips of card which can simply be glued into position ③. Use genuine colours for realism, or introduce a variety of colours if you want a more dramatic effect. Hook the ladder rungs over the branches to hang them from the tree.

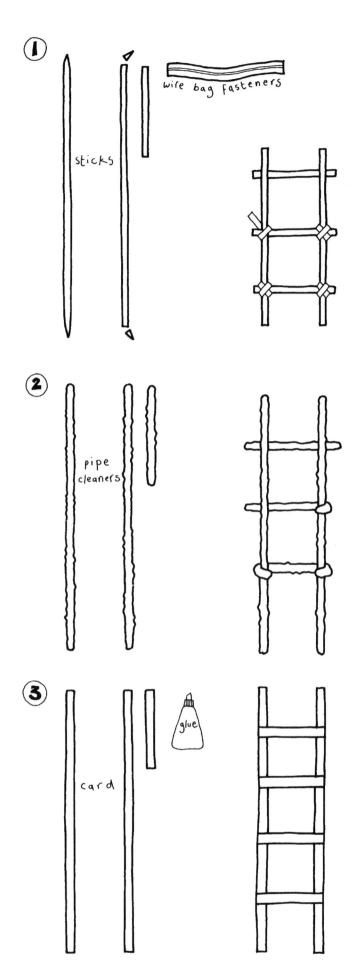

26

Joseph feeds God's people

Joseph was sold into slavery in Egypt by his brothers because they were jealous of him. God took care of him, and when the Pharaoh, who was ruler of Egypt, saw that God's favour rested on him, he made Joseph governor over all of his lands.

Then a terrible famine came, and nothing grew in the land of Canaan where Joseph's family lived. The people of Egypt did not go hungry because Joseph had explained God's warning dreams to Pharaoh, and the people had saved their crops for seven plentiful years. When Joseph's brothers heard that there was food in Egypt, they set off there because they were starving.

Bowing down before Joseph, they did not recognise him, although he knew who they were. Joseph sold them the food they wanted, and they returned to their father Jacob in Canaan. Before long, however, they grew hungry again, so once more they set out for Egypt. This time Joseph told them who he was. After the shock had worn off, they were afraid of what he might do to them, because of their cruel treatment of him so many years before.

But Joseph said to them, 'There is nothing to fear. Everything that has happened is God's will, so that I could save you from this famine.'

He kissed and hugged his brothers and sent them home to tell their father that his son Joseph was alive. Soon afterwards, Jacob and his sons moved to Egypt where the Pharaoh made them welcome, and Joseph took good care of them.

Adapted from Genesis 41:37-45:20

Joseph was the son of Jacob and Rachel, and his father's favourite child. Even when his brothers had plotted to get rid of him, God took care of Joseph and made sure that he came to no real harm. Joseph always stayed close to God; he did not misuse the power given to him by the Pharaoh, and he did not seek revenge against his brothers. Instead, he forgave those who had done him harm, and made sure that the 'children of Israel' did not suffer or starve. Through Joseph, God took care of his chosen people.

Wheat is the symbol for this story. Bunches of dried wheat are readily available from dried flower shops, most department stores and many garden centres. Once you have your wheat, you can decide how you are going to use it.

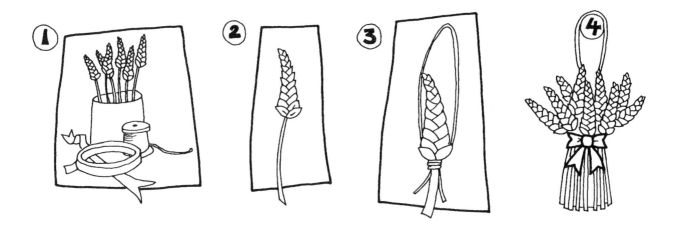

Wheat sheaves

1. You will need . . .

- Bunch of wheat
- Sellotape
- Gold thread
- Elastic band
- Narrow ribbon

For each sheaf of wheat, 6-8 stems should be sufficient. Using sellotape, attach a loop of gold thread at the top of one stem just below the ear ③. With this stem in the middle, arrange the others around it to produce an attractive bundle with the thread emerging from the middle. Trim off the lower half of the stems and use an elastic band to hold them together. Wrap a piece of narrow ribbon around to disguise the elastic band, and tie a bow ④. Now trim off any surplus lengths of stem to complete the sheaf.

2. You will need . . .

- Squares of felt, scrap material or crepe paper
- Glue
- Bunch of wheat
- Cotton wool (or other material suitable for stuffing)
- Gold thread

Cut a rectangular shape for the sack from the material of your choice. Fold it in half by bringing the shorter sides together ②. Glue the edges together leaving an opening at the top. Depending on the size of your sack, make a wheat sheaf of appropriate size as described above, using an elastic band to hold the stems together. Cut the stems so that they fit inside the sack with the ears protruding from the top. If necessary stuff the sack to make it appear full ③. Tie some gold thread tightly around the top of the sack, and make a loop so that the sack is ready to hang ④.

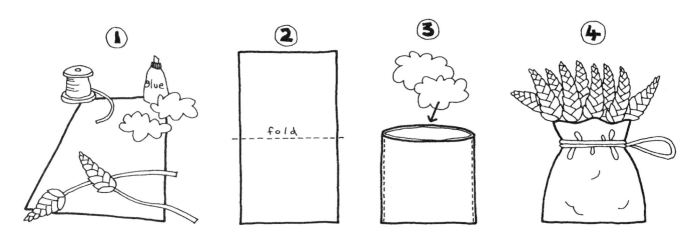

28

Moses leads the people out of Egypt

At first the Pharaoh allowed Moses to lead the Israelites out of Egypt, then once more he hardened his heart and sent his army and chariots to bring the people back. As the Israelites hurried away, the Egyptians gave chase, and when they reached the banks of the sea everything seemed lost.

As the people cried out with fear, Moses told them, 'Have courage, God will save us.'

God told Moses to stretch out his staff, and, as Moses did so, the waters of the sea parted and a dry path appeared before them. Quickly the people followed Moses through the sea, for Pharaoh's army was close behind them. When they reached the other side, Moses stretched out his staff again and the mighty walls of water closed over the Egyptians and they disappeared beneath the waves. God had saved his people, and the Israelites praised him and put their trust in Moses his servant.

Adapted from Exodus 14:10-31

Moses was another of the great leaders of the Israelites. At God's command he defied the Pharaoh and led the people from slavery in Egypt to the promised land. Moses was strong and courageous, and did whatever God commanded, because he had complete faith and trust in him. Moses used a staff to make a path through the sea, and this is his symbol on the Jesse tree.

Staff

You will need . . .

- Wire coat hanger or wire of similar thickness
- Brown ribbon, material or tissue paper
- Glue
- Newspaper, glue and brown poster paint (optional)
- Gold thread

Method 1

Cut a length of wire approx 16 cm long and bend one end round to make the handle of the staff. This can then be covered by wrapping ribbon or strips of material or paper round the wire, and gluing them into place ①. Alternatively, use strips of papier-mâché in the same way (see page 12) and paint the staff when dry ②. Whichever method of preparation you choose, don't forget to attach a loop of gold thread during the wrapping process for hanging the staff from the tree.

Method 2

Roll lengths of salt dough (see page 10 for recipe and instructions) into staff shapes ③. (These could be made at the same time as the apples described on page 10.) Use a cocktail stick to pierce a hole for hanging before slow baking in the oven and then painting.

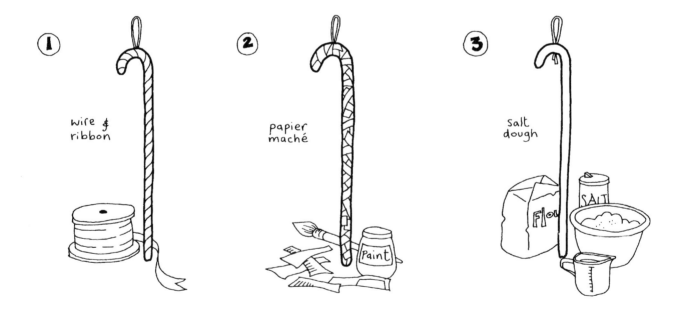

① wire & ribbon

② papier mâché

③ salt dough

Moses and the Ten Commandments

God called Moses to the top of Mount Sinai to speak to him. He gave Moses Ten Commandments telling his people how they must love God and love their neighbour.

1. I am the Lord your God, and you shall have no other before me.
2. You shall not worship any statues or other images.
3. You shall not use the Lord's name without reverence and respect.
4. You shall keep the Sabbath day holy.
5. You shall respect your mother and your father.
6. You shall not kill other people.
7. You shall not be unfaithful to your husband or your wife.
8. You shall not steal.
9. You shall not speak falsely about other people.
10. You shall not envy or desire what belongs to someone else.

Adapted from Exodus 20:1-17

God wrote the Ten Commandments on tablets of stone and gave them to Moses and his people to keep, so that the Israelites might live at peace with him and each other. God spoke to Moses face to face and made a covenant with him to always be with his people (Exodus 24:4-8). The Ten Commandments are symbolised by tablets of stone.

Stone tablets

You will need . . .

- Polystyrene pieces or tiles*
- Stanley knife
- Grey poster paint
- Cocktail stick
- Black felt-tip pen
- Gold thread

Carefully use a sharp Stanley knife to cut out two blocks of polystyrene approximately the same size (5 x 7 cm). If using thin tiles, you can glue several tiles together to give them greater depth. Don't worry about making your tablets too neat because, once painted, any irregularities add to the effect ②. Paint the tablets grey, and when dry, make a hole through the top using a cocktail stick. Use a fine-nibbed felt-tip pen to 'write' some words on each stone tablet ③. Then thread the gold thread through each tablet so that they can be hung in pairs ④.

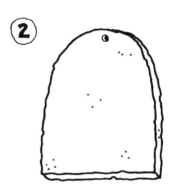

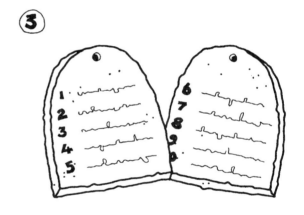

* A variety of materials could be used to make Moses' tablets of stone, but polystyrene is both light and gives an ideal 'stony' texture. Polystyrene tiles can be purchased from any DIY store, or save some pieces which have been used as a packing material.

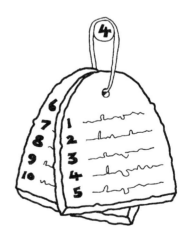

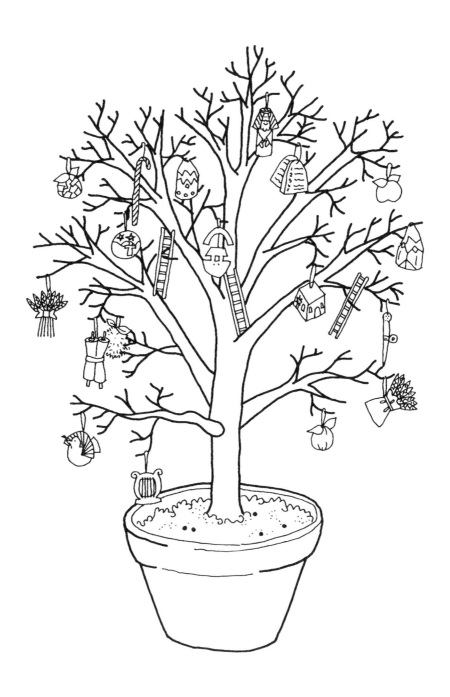

WEEK THREE

Isaiah's prophecy
Bethlehem house
King David the harpist
King Solomon

Isaiah's prophecy

The prophet Isaiah foretold: 'Just as new shoots sprout from the stump of a tree that has been cut down, so a new king will appear among the descendants of Jesse. God's spirit will rest on him, and he will be wise and all powerful.'

Adapted from Isaiah 11:1-2

Isaiah preached in Jerusalem between 740 and 700 BC. He was both a poet and a politician, but above all he was a prophet. A prophet is someone who speaks in the name of the Lord and sees everything according to God's plans. Isaiah was called to be a prophet after God appeared to him in a vision in the Temple, and he exerted considerable influence. Isaiah realised that salvation lies in faith and putting yourself completely in the hands of God. He believed in and foretold the coming of the true son of David, promised by God, a saviour who would one day come to establish universal peace and love. The fulfilment of Isaiah's prophecy is symbolised by a scroll.

Scroll

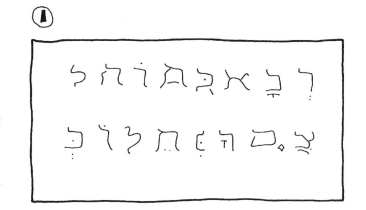

You will need . . .

- Sheets of white paper or baking parchment (divided into lengths 5 cm x 10 cm)
- Double-sided sellotape
- Wooden cocktail sticks (trimmed) or wooden dowel cut into short lengths
- Narrow ribbon

Copy the scroll on to paper or, for a more authentic look, on to some baking parchment, and cut to size ①. Wrap a 5 cm length of double-sided sellotape around the middle of two trimmed cocktail sticks ②. Lay the paper or parchment flat (writing side up) and carefully position a cocktail stick at each short end. Press the sellotaped stick down onto the paper and carefully begin to roll inwards ③. A piece of ribbon sellotaped to one side can be used for fastening the scroll and hanging it from the tree ④.

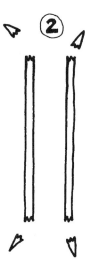

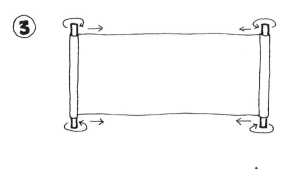

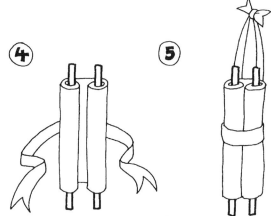

Bethlehem house

God sent Samuel to Bethlehem to find a man called Jesse. 'I have chosen a king from among Jesse's sons,' God said.

When Samuel met Jesse and his seven sons, he thought to himself, 'Surely God has chosen one of these', for they were strong and handsome young men. But as Jesse introduced each of his sons, God said to Samuel, 'This is not the one.'

Finally Samuel asked Jesse, 'Do you have any more sons, because God has chosen none of these.'

'My youngest son, David, is watching over the sheep,' Jesse replied.

'Then send for him,' Samuel said.

As David, Jesse's youngest son, came running to meet Samuel, God spoke again, 'This is the chosen one!'

So Samuel anointed David with holy oil just as God had told him, and, from that day on, the spirit of God was with David.

Adapted from 1 Samuel 16:4-13

Jesse was a descendant of Abraham, who lived in a town called Bethlehem in Judea. God had chosen David, Jesse's youngest son, to be King Saul's successor and to lead the people of Israel. So it came to be that the saviour God had promised to send would be a descendant of Jesse's family who came from Bethlehem, their family home.

The symbol of the house is used to represent Bethlehem, the town where Jesse lived. Since the houses of the time had flat roofs, small boxes are ideal to hang from the tree. These can be purchased from card shops or made yourself, before adding details such as windows, doors or stairs.

House

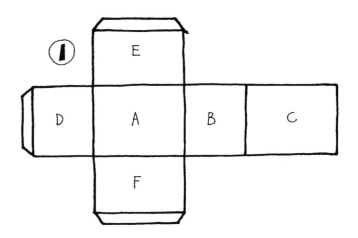

You will need . . .

- Small cardboard boxes (purchased ready made) or cartridge paper
- Gold thread
- Sellotape and glue
- White or coloured paper
- Felt-tip pens

If you are using ready-made boxes, open the lid of the box and make a small hole in the centre. Make a loop from the gold thread and push it through the lid, with the knot on the inside of the box. Close the lid and secure with sellotape. Cut out pieces of white or coloured paper for doors and windows, and use felt-tip pens to draw window frames, designs, etc. Glue these on to the sides of the house. Houses of the time often had an outdoor staircase to the roof, so add one of these to the side of the box.

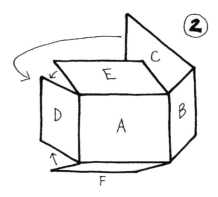

If you are making your own boxes, trace the pattern on page 61 and make a card template ①. Cut out the required number of 'houses' from coloured cartridge paper and score carefully along the lines. Fold into shape and glue the tabs in place ②. Make a small hole in the 'roof' of the house and pass a loop of gold thread through ③. Add appropriate details to complete the houses as described above ④.

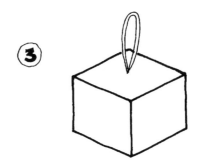

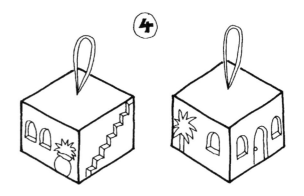

King David the harpist

King Saul was a troubled man and he told his servants, 'Find me someone who can play the harp well and bring him to me.' One of the servants knew that Jesse's youngest son, David, could play and sing well. So Saul sent messengers to Bethlehem to fetch David from his father's house. David became Saul's servant, and before long the king grew very fond of him. Whenever Saul was troubled, David would play his harp, and the beautiful music would soothe Saul and make him feel better.

Adapted from 1 Samuel 16:14-23

As the youngest of Jesse's sons, David was considered to be the least important, but God chose him to lead his people. David united the tribes of Israel into one kingdom, and made Jerusalem his capital city. There he brought the Ark of the Covenant (the holy resting-place of the Ten Commandments) and made plans to build a magnificent Temple for the Lord. God promised David that his descendants would be a continuous royal line.

King David was known as the 'sweet psalmist of Israel' and is believed to have written many of the songs and poems which we call psalms, to praise and honour God. He is symbolised on the Jesse tree by his harp.

Large department stores and shops selling Christmas decorations do have a variety of harp decorations suitable for hanging on a tree, if you don't want to make your own.

Harp

You will need . . .

- Gold card
- Darning needle
- Gold thread
- Double-sided sellotape
- Thick white card
- Gold spray paint

Trace the harp pattern on page 62 to make a template **(1)**. Unless the card is gold on both sides, you will need to cut two pieces of card for each decoration.

Take one half of the harp and carefully push the needle through from one side to the other. Aim to make five holes at the top and five at the bottom. Thread the needle with a length of gold thread, and, starting at the top, pass the needle from the back of the card through the hole **(2)**, and back through the corresponding hole at the bottom (see diagram). Take care not to pull the thread all the way through, by securing approximately 1 cm of thread with a small piece of sellotape **(3)**. Continue to pass the needle from back to front until all the holes have been threaded **(4)**. Make sure the 'strings' are taut before finally cutting and sticking the end in place as before. Stick double-sided sellotape on to the back of the other half of the harp. Fold a piece of gold thread in half and press the ends together on to the sellotape at the top of the harp to make a loop. Now carefully position the two halves together and press firmly **(5)**.

Alternatively, use ordinary thick white card and cut out and thread as described above. Put a hole in the top, and spray the harp with gold paint, before adding a loop of gold thread to hang the decoration.

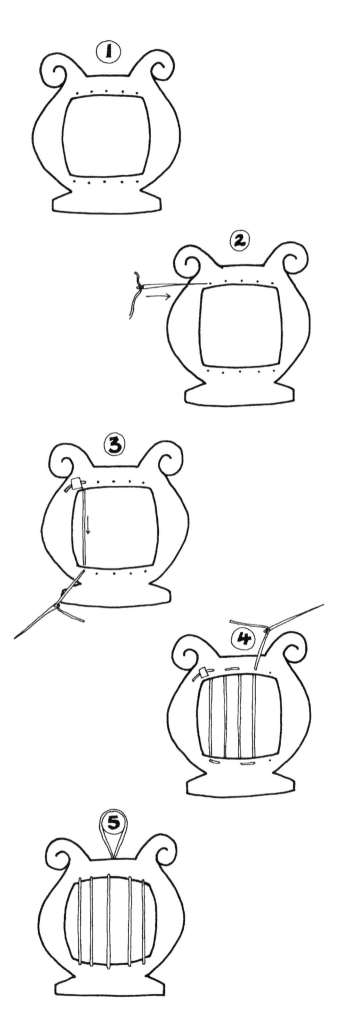

King Solomon

When David died, his son Solomon became king, and God promised Solomon that he would give him wisdom and understanding to make him a great king.

One day two women appeared before Solomon and asked him to settle their argument. Each woman had recently had a baby, but one of the children had died and both women now claimed that the surviving child was theirs. The women argued bitterly and fought over the child.

So Solomon said, 'Fetch my sword and I will settle this by cutting the child in two.'

'What a good idea,' said one of the women. 'Then neither of us can have him!'

But the other woman cried out, 'No, don't hurt him! I will give him away rather than see him harmed.'

King Solomon then knew that this woman was the baby's true mother, and he gave the child to her. When the people heard about Solomon's wise judgement, they were filled with admiration and respect, for they knew that such wisdom was indeed given to him by God.

Adapted from 1 Kings 3:16-28

Solomon was King David's son, and was renowned for his great wisdom. He is said to have written many wise sayings, and is believed to be the author of much of the book of Proverbs. Under Solomon's wise kingship, the Israelites enjoyed peace and prosperity. As his father had planned, Solomon spent seven years building the magnificent Temple where the people worshipped God, and it became central to the life of Israel.

The symbol for kingship is a crown. Again, crown decorations are readily available to buy, but just as easy to make yourself. Two simple ideas are suggested.

Crown 1

You will need . . .

- Gold or coloured card
- Sellotape
- Glue
- Sequins, beads, crumpled foil wrappers or glitter for decoration
- Gold thread

Trace the pattern on page 62 to make a template from gold or coloured card and cut out the number of crown shapes you need ①. Use sellotape to stick the ends together, and then glue the decorations into place. Cut a piece of gold thread (approximately 16 cm long) and sellotape each end to the inside of the crown so that it can be hung from the tree ②.

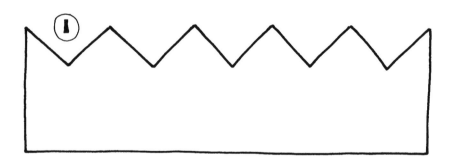

Crown 2

You will need . . .

- Four 15 cm squares of coloured paper
- Double-sided sellotape
- Gold thread
- Glue
- Sequins, beads, crumpled foil wrappers or glitter for decoration

Take a square of paper and, with the white side up, turn it so that the corner is facing you. Now fold the bottom corner (facing you) to meet the top corner (opposite you) ②. Gently fold the long edge in half to find the middle ③, then firmly fold the pointed corners into that middle point ④. Repeat with a second square of coloured paper and stand them opposite each other with their corners pointing together ⑤. Next slot the corner of each triangle inside the other, making sure that the folds meet ⑥. Use sellotape to secure the corners and some gold thread for hanging the crowns. Decorate the crowns with sequins and beads or by simply turning down the corner to reveal white diamonds ⑧. Adapt the size of the crowns by using smaller or larger paper squares, or by adding more squares.

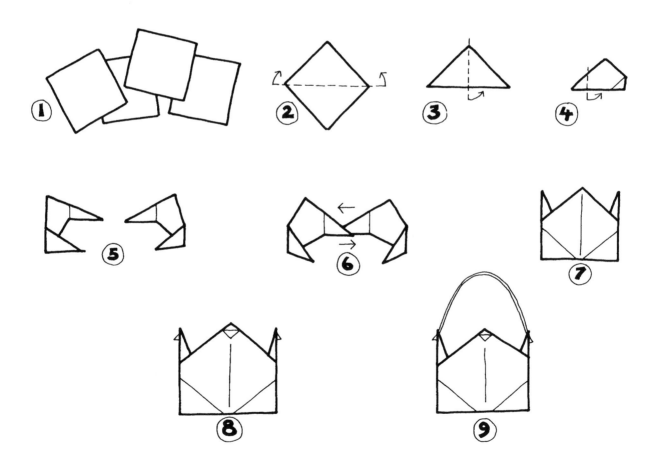

WEEK FOUR

Joseph the carpenter
Mary the mother of Jesus
John the Baptist
Jesus, Saviour of the world

Joseph the carpenter

Mary was engaged to Joseph the carpenter, but before they were married Mary told Joseph that she was expecting a baby. Joseph, who was a good and kind man, wanted to protect Mary from gossip and scandal, so he decided to break off their engagement quietly.

One night as he slept, an angel appeared to him and said, 'Joseph, descendant of King David, do not be afraid to take Mary as your wife. This child has been conceived by the Holy Spirit, and Mary will have a son and you will call him Jesus.'

When Joseph awoke, he did as the angel had said and took Mary to be his wife. When the time came she gave birth to a son and they named him Jesus just as the angel had told them.

Adapted from Matthew 1:18-25

Like his ancestors before him, Joseph had great faith and trust in God. He was a just and honourable man who bore the responsibilities of a father perfectly. He was with Mary when Jesus was born, and, when the wise men came to worship the new-born child, they found Joseph taking care of him. He took Mary and Jesus to Egypt when the angel warned him of King Herod's plans, and protected them from harm. He took Jesus as a baby to be presented in the Temple, and shared Mary's fears when twelve-year-old Jesus seemed to be lost in Jerusalem.

Joseph was a craftsman by trade, and probably taught Jesus the skills of a carpenter. The tree decorations suggested for his character are a hammer and saw which are quick and easy to make.

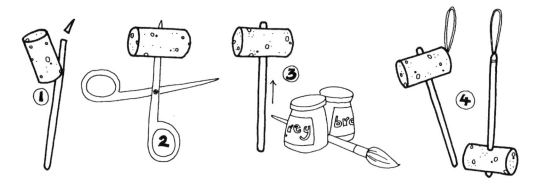

Hammer

You will need . . .

- Corks
- Corkscrew or scissors
- Wooden kebab sticks (trimmed) or narrow dowel rod (approx 9 cm lengths)
- Grey and brown poster paints
- Gold thread
- Drawing pin (optional)

Make a hole through the middle of a cork using a corkscrew or sharp pair of scissors ②. Paint the cork grey and the wooden stick brown and allow to dry. Attach the handle by carefully pushing the stick through the cork allowing about 0.5 cm to protrude through to the other side ③. To hang from the tree use a loop of gold thread which can be attached to the cork with a drawing pin, or alternatively use scissors to make a groove at the end of the hammer handle and tie the thread firmly round this ④.

Saw

You will need . . .

- Thin white card
- Brown felt-tip pens
- Small pointed scissors
- Wooden cocktail sticks
- Grey felt-tip pen or silver paint marker pen (optional)
- Double-sided sellotape
- Gold thread

Cut two lengths of card 1 x 8 cm. Take one piece, colour it brown on both sides, and mark a point 1 cm from each end. Using sharp pointed scissors, carefully make a small hole at each mark ①. Then take the second length of card. Colour it grey or silver and allow it to dry before cutting a zig-zag along one side of its length to make the blade of the saw ②. Push cocktail sticks through the holes on the first piece and trim off the pointed ends. Leave about 1.5 cm of stick protruding through the card ③. Wrap a narrow strip of double-sided sellotape around each cocktail stick about 2 cm from the end, then press the ends of the 'saw' on to the tape. Complete by attaching a loop of gold thread to one of the cocktail sticks ④.

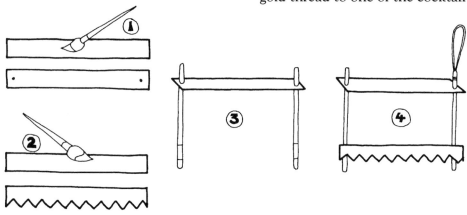

Mary, the mother of Jesus

God sent the angel Gabriel to a town in Galilee called Nazareth, to a young woman there called Mary. She was engaged to marry a carpenter called Joseph, a descendant of King David's family.

The angel greeted Mary with the words, 'Be glad, Mary, for God is with you and has given you great blessings.'

Mary was troubled and wondered what the angel's words meant.

'There is nothing to fear,' Gabriel assured her. 'You will have a son and name him Jesus. He will be called Son of the Most High, whose reign will never end.'

'How can this happen,' asked Mary, 'when I am not married?'

'The Holy Spirit will come to you,' said Gabriel. 'This child will be holy and be known as the Son of God.'

Then Mary knelt before the angel and said, 'I am God's servant, and will do whatever he asks. Let everything happen just as you have said.'

Then the angel left her and Mary found herself alone.

Adapted from Luke 1:26-38

When Mary learned that she had been chosen to give birth to the Son of God, she rejoiced and praised God. God chose a daughter of Israel to be the mother of his son. At the angel's announcement, Mary responded with the obedience of faith, with complete confidence that nothing is impossible for God. By giving her consent to God's word, Mary agreed to be the mother of God's Son, and brought to fulfilment the divine promise given through the prophet Isaiah: 'Behold, a virgin will conceive and bear a son.' (Isaiah 7:14)

Mary the mother of Jesus is symbolised by a white rose, a beautiful flower which represents her purity and sinless perfection. You could use artificial roses and attach them to the branches with wire or thread, or make your own flowers using tissue paper.

Rose

You will need . . .

- Squares of white tissue paper (15 x 15 cm)
- Sticky tape
- Wire bag closers
- Gold thread (optional)

Take a square of tissue paper and turn it so that a corner is facing you. Then place another square on top at an angle to form the shape of an eight-pointed star ①. Holding the two pieces of tissue paper together, place your index finger in the middle and carefully scrunch the paper up and around it. Twist the paper in the middle into a stem which is held in place with a piece of sticky tape ②. Wind a wire bag closer around the 'flower stem' to attach the flower to the tree ③, or group several flowers together in a posy and hang this from the tree using a loop of gold thread ④.

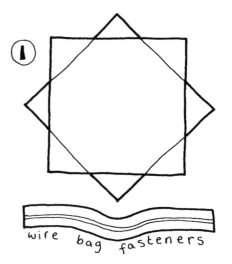

wire bag fasteners

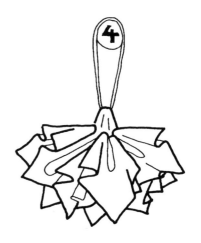

John the Baptist

Zechariah's wife Elizabeth gave birth to a son, and their friends and family celebrated God's kindness to them for they were both elderly. When the baby was a week old, the time came to take him to the Temple according to the law.

The people there said, 'Surely they will call him Zechariah after his father', but Elizabeth spoke up and said, 'His name will be John!'

'But there is no one in your family with that name!' they exclaimed, and they turned to Zechariah to ask his opinion.

Because Zechariah had earlier been struck dumb by an angel, he had to write down these words: 'His name is John!'

At that very moment his speech returned, and, filled with the Holy Spirit, he said:

'Praise the God of Israel
for he has set his people free.
He has sent a Saviour, a descendant from
    the house of David.
He has remembered his promise to Abraham
    to rescue us.
And you, my child, will be called a prophet
    of God.
You will go before the Lord and prepare a
    path for him,
telling his people that they will be saved
through the forgiveness of their sins.'

John grew strong in body and spirit, and went to live in the desert until the time came for him to begin preaching.

Adapted from Luke 1:57-80

John the Baptist was the son of Mary's elderly cousin Elizabeth, who had been childless for many years. From the moment the angel appeared to Zechariah, and told him that he would have a son whose name would be John, it was obvious that John had been sent by God. He was filled with the Holy Spirit and came to prepare the people for the coming of the Saviour Jesus. Many people who confessed their sins to him were baptised in the River Jordan, and so John became known as the 'Baptist'. After baptising Jesus, John told his disciples to follow the 'Lamb of God'. When he spoke out bravely against King Herod, John was imprisoned and finally put to death.

Zechariah had been struck dumb because he did not believe the angel Gabriel's message that he would have a son (Luke 1:11-20). So when the child was born and people asked him what he wanted to name his son, Zechariah had to write his answer down for them. He probably wrote on paper made from papyrus using a reed pen dipped in ink. John's symbol is a writing board made with parchment, and a reed pen.

Writing board and pen

You will need . . .

- Thin brown card (or white card coloured brown)
- Baking parchment
- Black biro pen
- Glue stick
- Cocktail sticks
- Black felt-tip pen
- Gold thread
- Sellotape

Make a template from the pattern on page 62 and cut a writing board from the card ①. Measure a piece of baking parchment 5 x 5 cm and tear along the edges to give the paper a rough, uneven finish ②. Write the words 'His name is John' with a black biro pen, before wrapping the top of the parchment around the pen to make it curl ③. Glue the middle of the parchment on to the writing board at an angle, leaving the edges free ④ and taking care to make sure that the writing is the right way up when you hang the board from the tree! Cut the cocktail stick in half, and use a felt-tip pen to colour the pointed tip black to make the writing reed ⑤. Glue one side and stick it on to the parchment. Make a loop of gold thread and sellotape it to the back of the handle to hang ⑥.

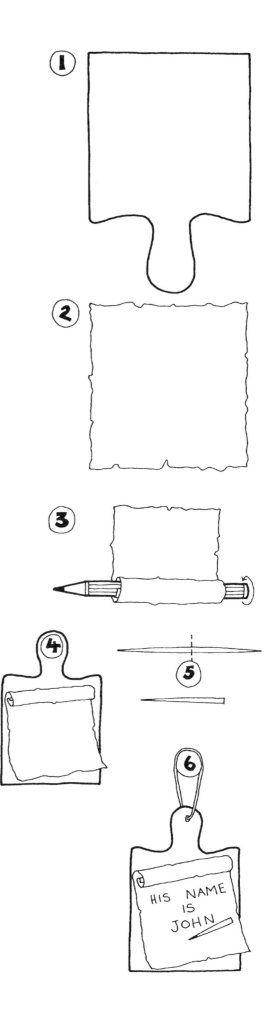

Jesus, Saviour of the world

When the time came for Mary to have her child, she gave birth to a son and they named him Jesus. Three wise men had seen his star rise in the heavens, and they followed it because they wanted to worship the new-born king. The sight of the star filled them with joy, as it hung in the sky above the place where Jesus lay. Going in, they saw the child with his mother Mary, and they fell to their knees and worshipped him.

So it came to be that the Saviour God had promised to his faithful people was born in Bethlehem in Judea just as the prophets had foretold:

> For you, Bethlehem in the Land of Judah,
> are by no means unimportant
> for from you a leader will come
> for my people Israel
> whose ancestors can be traced to ancient days.
> (Micah 5:2)

Adapted from Matthew 1:25; 2:9-11

Jesus, our Saviour and the Light of the World, was born in Bethlehem, the city of David, in a place marked out by a shining star. Suitable stars are readily available in department stores, or you can make them yourself.

Star

You will need . . .

- Thin gold or silver card (Alternatively, paint card with gold or silver spray paint, or cover with aluminium foil or silver wrapping paper)
- Hole punch
- Gold thread
- Glitter, sequins and glue (optional)

Trace the star shape on page 62 and make a template for cutting out stars from gold and/or silver card ①. Punch holes and thread with loops of gold thread to hang ②. Decorate with glitter or sequins before hanging from the tree ③.

Ideally, if practical, this should be done on Christmas Day to complete the Jesse tree.

glitter   sequins

TEMPLATES

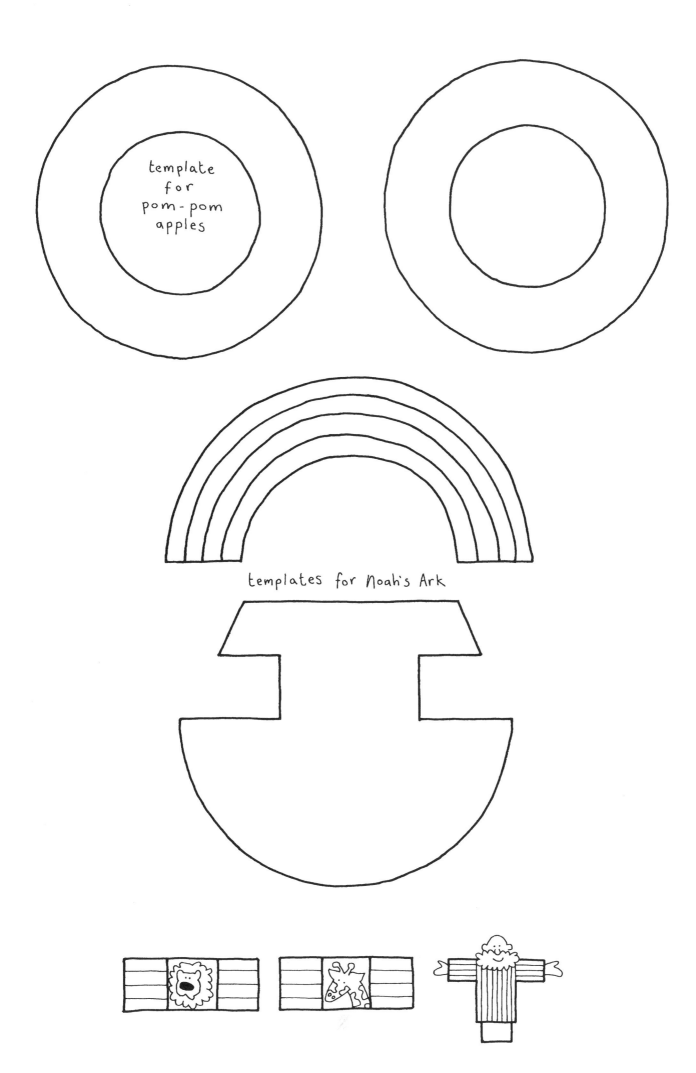

template
for
pom-pom
apples

templates for Noah's Ark

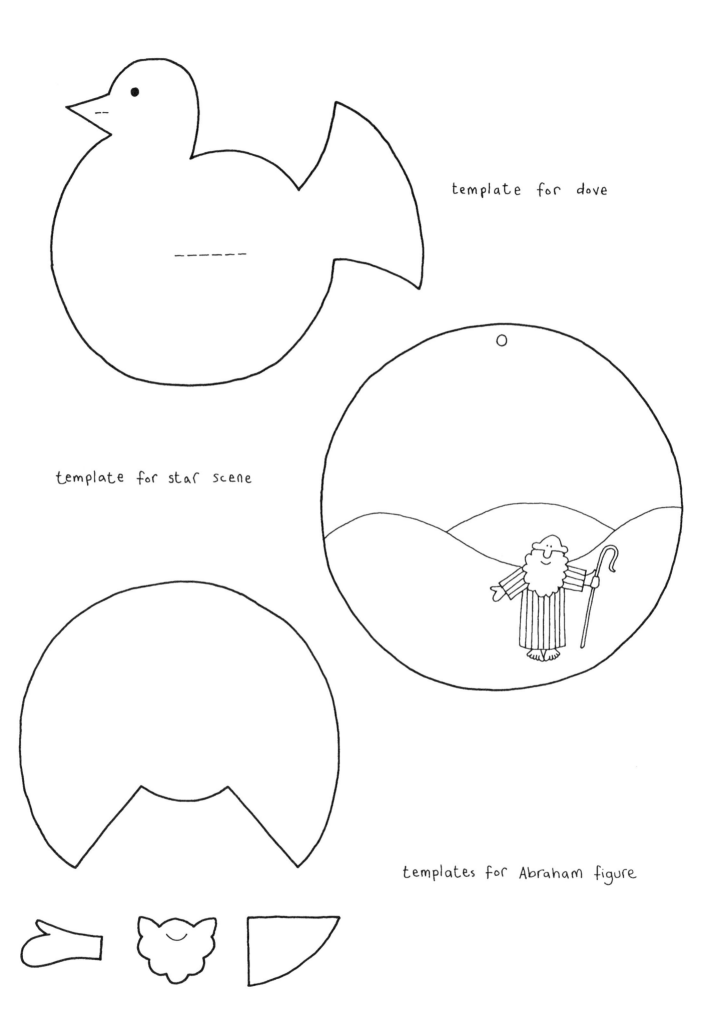

template for dove

template for star scene

templates for Abraham figure

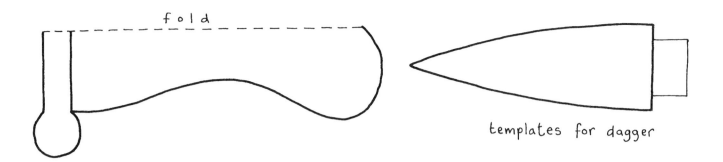

fold

templates for dagger

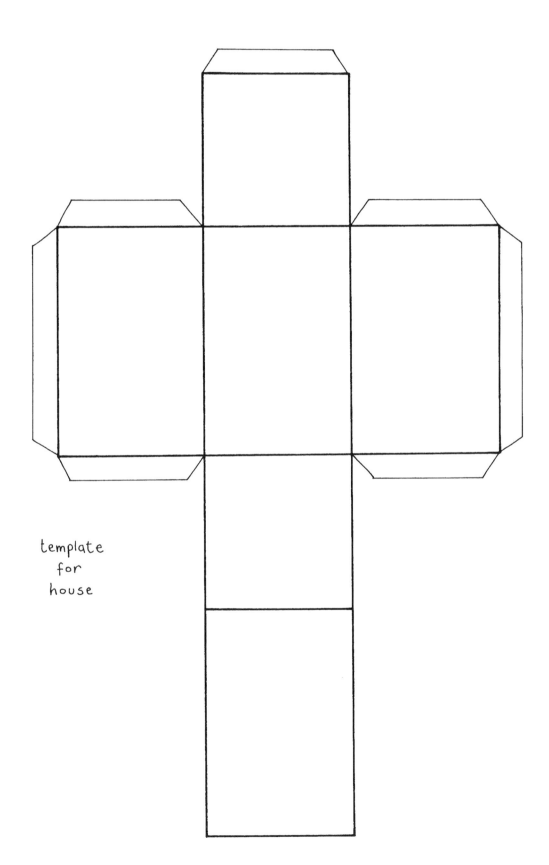

template
for
house

template
for
harp

template for crown

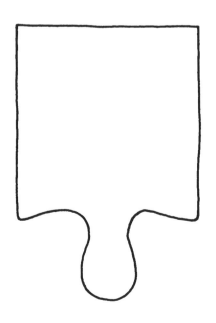

template for
writing board

template
for
star